THE BATTLE OF WATERLOO

The Battle that Changed Europe Forever

Written by Gaëtan Deghilage
In collaboration with Mélanie Mettra
Translated by Carly Probert

History   50MINUTES.com

THE BATTLE OF WATERLOO

KEY INFORMATION

- **When:** 18 June 1815
- **Where:** Waterloo (Belgium)
- **Context:** The Napoleonic Wars (1803-1815)
- **Belligerents:** The French Empire against the United Kingdom, the Kingdom of Prussia, the United Kingdom of the Netherlands and various small German states.
- **Commanders and leaders:**
  - Gebhard Leberecht Blücher, Prussian marshal (1742-1819)
  - Napoleon I, French emperor (1769-1821)
  - Arthur Wellesley, Duke of Wellington, commander of British, Dutch and German troops (1769-1852)
- **Outcome:** Decisive victory of the coalition
- **Victims:**
  - French camp: approximately 26 000 killed and wounded
  - Coalition camp: approximately 24 000 killed and wounded

INTRODUCTION

Napoleon I came to power in France in 1799 and, during his reign, tried to control the entire European continent, prompting the creation of several coalitions of the major European powers of the time (the United Kingdom, Prussia, Russia and Austria) against him.

Defeated for the first time in 1814, Napoleon returned to power a year later and raised a new army. Hoping to triumph over his opponents before they joined forces against him, he invaded Belgium on 15 June in order to defeat the British, the Dutch and the Prussians. A French victory would revive the Empire and plunge Europe into war once again; a defeat would mark the end of the Napoleonic era and the return of the monarchy in France: this challenge was therefore crucial.

The battle took place on 18 June in Mont-Saint-Jean, a few kilometers south of Waterloo. At 11:15am, Napoleon I risked everything and attacked. The Anglo-Dutch army, under the command of Arthur Wellesley, managed to contain the French and, a few hours later, gained the reinforcement of the Prussian troops, commanded by Gebhard Leberecht Blücher. The allies attacked and the French were beaten and forced to flee.

The victory was decisive: Napoleon abdicated a second time on 22 June 1815 and was exiled to the island of St. Helena (South Atlantic).

POLITICAL AND SOCIAL CONTEXT

Far from being an isolated event, the Battle of Waterloo was the end point of a struggle between revolutionary, and then imperial, France and the other European powers who felt threatened by the expansionist ambitions of Napoleon I. To understand the origins of this conflict, we must look back at the French Revolution (1789).

THE WARS OF THE FRENCH REVOLUTION, A PRELUDE TO THE NAPOLEONIC WARS

Although in 1789 the French people revolted to express their dissatisfaction with the imbalances of society, the Revolution quickly radicalized and pushed European rulers, who feared that it would spread to their own territories, to react. There were several threats to the movement, but they only served to strengthen it: after heavy battle, the Republic was proclaimed on 21 September 1792 and King Louis XVI (1754-1793) was imprisoned, tried and executed on 21 January 1793.

Instead of coming to an end, the conflict strengthened and became ideological: the aim of the new regime in place was to extend the revolution to other European nations to bring them freedom, while the sovereigns wanted to conquer the Republic in order to prevent revolutionary ideas from threatening their kingdoms. Therefore, the different states came together to create coalitions that France had to measure up to:

- The first coalition, formed in 1793, included Great Britain, Austria, Prussia, the United Provinces (the Netherlands), Spain and Russia. The fighting lasted until 1797 and resulted in a victory for France, which even managed to conquer the Austrian Low Countries (Belgium) and the left bank of the Rhine. The Republic also entered into an alliance with Spain and extended its influence to Northern Italy;
- The second coalition, formed in 1798, brought together mainly Britain, Russia and Austria. While the coalition initially seemed able to win, they split again and France emerged from the conflict victorious. In 1801 and 1802, a series of treaties were signed between the allies and France that formalized the annexation of Belgium and the left bank of the Rhine and increased its influence in Italy.

DID YOU KNOW?

During that time, the map of Europe was not like the one we know today:

- Germany was not unified and was thus divided into many small states dominated by Austria in the south and Prussia in the east. Unification did not happen until 1871;
- Italy was also fragmented. The country was not united until 1870;
- Belgium belonged to Austria until the French conquest in 1794. After the defeat of Napoleon I, it was attached to the United Provinces to form

the United Kingdom of the Netherlands. But the union did not last and the Belgians acquired their independence in 1830. This is why we refer to Dutch soldiers to designate the Dutch and the Belgians.

THE FRENCH EMPIRE, FROM VICTORIES TO NUMEROUS SETBACKS

During the coup of 18 Brumaire (a name from the revolutionary calendar, corresponding to 9 November 1799), Napoleon Bonaparte took power in France. This episode marked the end of the Republic and the beginning of the Consulate, an authoritarian regime headed by the First Consul, who took the name of Napoleon I. He further strengthened his power when he proclaimed himself emperor on 18 May 1804. Although the ideological aspect of the conflict between France and the other European powers gradually lost its importance, the war continued because of Napoleon's expansionist ambitions:

• The War of the Third Coalition (1805) between France and the United Kingdom, Russia and Austria. While the English won an important battle at Trafalgar (21 October), the Russians and the Austrians were severely beaten on the continent, especially in Austerlitz (2 December). This defeat proved fatal to the Austrians who withdrew from the war. The alliance was dissolved;

On 2 December 1805, in Austerlitz (now Slavkov u Brna, Czech Republich), Napoleon I, at the head of 75 000 men, faced 90 000 Austro-Russians. Faced with superior forces, the Emperor achieved one of his most impressive victories: there were only 5 500 of the French dead or injured, compared to the 16 000 enemies incapacitated, 10 000 prisoners and 185 artillery pieces captured.

A few weeks earlier, on 21 October 1805, off Cape Trafalgar (Spain), the Franco-Spanish fleet of 33 ships commanded by Vice Admiral Pierre-Charles Silvestre de Villeneuve (1763-1806), met that of the British, composed of 27 ships and commanded by Vice Admiral Horatio Nelson (1758-1805). Despite Nelson's death, the clash ended in a decisive victory for Great Britain.

The Battle of Austerlitz and the Battle of Trafalgar can be seen as the assertion of the dominance of France and Britain on their preferred terrain: the first preferring the land, the second preferring the sea.

- The War of the Fourth Coalition (1806-1807) mainly the saw the French facing the Prussians. The Prussians were quickly beaten in September 1806 and, like the Austrians the previous year, were forced to leave the coalition. The Russians were defeated in early 1808 and Emperor Alexander I (1777-1825) was forced to ally with Napoleon I.

- The War of the Fifth Coalition began with the British intervention in the Iberian Peninsula (1808) to support a revolt against the French occupiers. Taking this opportunity, the Austrians revived their war against France, but were beaten during the summer of 1809. After these victories, the French Empire reached its peak: it covered France, Belgium, the Netherlands, part of Germany and Italy. Moreover, Napoleon controlled Spain, the Rhine States (Germany) and Poland, and was an ally of Prussia and Austria.

- The War of the Sixth Coalition began in 1812, when the French emperor invaded Russia with the *Grande Armée* (consisting of about 650 000 men). Moscow fell to the French in September, but Alexander I refused to negotiate. The Russians set fire to the capital, forcing Napoleon I into a difficult retreat. Meanwhile, Arthur Wellesley (the future Duke of Wellington) forced the French to leave Spain. Taking advantage of the French defeat, Austria and Prussia joined the coalition. Together they inflicted several major defeats on Napoleon I, who abdicated at Fontainebleau on 6 April 1814.

THE HUNDRED DAYS

Following his abdication and the signing of the Treaty of Fontainebleau (11th April 1814), Napoleon was exiled to the island of Elba (located off the coast of Tuscany, Italy) which was ceded to him in full sovereignty, while the monarchy was restored in France: Louis XVIII (1755-1824), brother of Louis XVI, ascended to the throne.

However, Napoleon I was not ready to give up and returned to France a few months later with the goal of regaining power. On 1 March 1815, he docked in the South East of France; this date marks the beginning of the Hundred Days that correspond to the last period of his reign. Thus began his ascent to Paris, during which time each troop sent to stop him rallied in his army. Finally, on 20 March, he entered the capital from which Louis XVIII had fled and took refuge in the United Kingdom of the Netherlands.

Upon his return, Napoleon I reorganized the French armies so as to support the war he knew was inevitable against the coalition. Besides men in garrison, he managed to mobilize a field army of approximately 210 000 soldiers. But on the other side, the seventh coalition was forming and was composed of troops vastly superior in number to his. The alliance included:

- 100 000 Anglo-Dutch in Western Belgium, commanded by Arthur Wellesley;
- 150 000 Prussians in Eastern Belgium and Luxemburg, commanded by Gebhard Leberecht Blücher;
- 300 000 Austrians along the Rhine and in Italy, commanded by Karl Philipp, Prince of Schwarzenberg (1771-1820);
- 165 000 Russians marching to France, commanded by Michael Andreas Barclay de Tolly (1761-1818).

Instead of waiting for the invasion of this huge army, Napoleon decided to take the lead: he wanted to attack in Belgium. His plan was to move towards Charleroi to conquer the vanguard of the Prussian army and then to turn against the British army stationed further north-west. He therefore hoped to defeat his two enemies separately, without them being able to regroup.

On 15 June 1815, Napoleon entered Belgium at the head of an army of approximately 125 000 men and, according to his plans, beat the Prussian troops stationed around Charleroi at the Battle of Ligny on 16 June. But, it was not until the next morning that the French emperor ordered Marshall Emmanuel, Marquis de Grouchy (1766-1847), to pursue the Prussians, allowing them to plan their retreat and face Arthur Wellesley later at Waterloo. Meanwhile, Napoleon entrusted to Marshal Michel Ney (1769-1815) the mission to attack the British positions at the crossroads of Quatre Bras, so as not to give them the opportunity to organize their defense. However, this failed and Arthur Wellesley had plenty of time to withdraw his troops to a previously recognized defense position, Mont-Saint-Jean, south of Waterloo. It was here that, on 18 June, the decisive battle marked the end of the Hundred Days.

GOOD TO KNOW

At Ligny, Napolean I directed approximately 60 000 men against 90 000 Prussians under the command of Gebhard Leberecht Blücher. The emperor won a total victory that allowed him to put almost 25 000 enemies out of action. Nevertheless, he lost about 7 000 men and did not bother to immediately pursue the Prussians, which would have adverse consequences in the following days.

As for French Marshal Michel Ney, he received the order to open the road to Brussels and cover the Emperor's attack against the Prussians by securing the Quatre Bras. There, he met a small Anglo-Dutch group (approximately 8 000 men), while he had at his disposal a little less than 30 000 men. But Michel Ney was slow to take action and during the confrontation that lasted all afternoon and part of the evening, the Allies were continually sent reinforcements, allowing them to keep the French in check. The meeting ended with a status quo. Only on learning of the Prussian defeat at Ligny did Arthur Wellesley decide to retreat to Waterloo.

COMMANDERS AND LEADERS

NAPOLEON I, FRENCH EMPEROR

Napoleon Bonaparte was born in Ajaccio (Corsica) on 15 August, 1769. Coming from the minor Corsican nobility, he received a military education during which he already showed a predisposition for command, including in simple snowball fights where he directed his classmates. In 1784, he was assigned to an infantry regiment.

The conflicts that broke out during the Revolution allowed him to gain fame in France, to take power and to try and extend French rule over the whole of Europe. Thus, during the War of the First Coalition, he was noted during the Italian campaigns for his bold strategies and his many victories, even though he had fewer men than his opponent. Becoming cumbersome for the members of the Directory (French regime, 1795-1799), he was sent to Egypt in order to personally implement his plan, which aimed to undermine Britain by cutting the route to India. Upon his return, Napoleon Bonaparte organized a coup and established the Consulate on 9 November 1799. As First Consul, he ran the country, ended the War of the Second Coalition and proclaimed himself Emperor of the French on 18 May 1804. This was followed by the wars of the third, fourth, fifth and sixth coalitions, justified by the fact that, in order to govern in peace, he first had to defeat his opponents, who wanted to destroy his plan and ensure that France became a monarchy state once again. Beaten and exiled first in 1814, Napoleon was definitively defeated in the Battle of Waterloo. He abdicated for a second time on 22 June 1815. Exiled on the island of St. Helena, he died there on 5 May 1821.

Limiting Napoleon I to his brilliant strategic mind is somewhat simplistic. Indeed, at the head of France, he made economic and administrative reforms and established a new civil code that still influences the laws of France and other European countries today. However, after his fall and exile, he left France partially ruined and demographically weakened.

ARTHUR WELLESLEY, COMMANDER OF BRITISH, DUTCH AND GERMAN TROOPS

Arthur Wellesley was born on 1 May 1769, probably in Dagan Castle (Ireland). After a conventional education for a young nobleman, he joined the army and took part in the War of the First Coalition. He was then sent to India, where he commanded his own division and successfully took part in several wars.

Following these success, Arthur Wellesley left for the Iberian Peninsula to support the rebellion against the French occupiers. Multiplying his victories, he drove the French from Portugal in 1810 and 1811, then pushed them out of Spain after the Battle of Vitoria (21 June 1813). He then led his troops to the South of France and contributed significantly to the defeat of Napoleon in 1814.

After being named Duke of Wellington, Arthur Wellesley was in Vienna to negotiate peace when the French emperor returned from exile. Aware of the threat he was under, Wellesley quickly returned to take command of the British forces in Belgium to face the French attack which began on 14 June. After the Prussian defeat at Ligny on 16 August, the Duke of Wellington retreated to Mont-Saint-Jean, a fortified position where he hoped to withstand the onslaught until the arrival of Prussian reinforcements. Everything happened as planned and on 18 June, Napoleon was defeated.

In addition to his military career, Arthur Wellesley also led a political career. During the war, he was a member of the House of Commons in Ireland, then in that of the UK. After the war, he held senior political and military positions, including that of Prime Minister of the United Kingdom between 1828 and 1830. He retired from politics in 1846 and died at Walmer Castle (England) on 14 September 1852.

GEBHARD LEBERECHT VON BLÜCHER

Glebhard Leberecht von Blücher was born in Rostock (Germany) on 16 December 1742. While participating in the Seven Years' War (1756-1763) on behalf on the Kingdom of Sweden, he was captured by the Prussian army in 1760 and forced to join. He served the Prussian King Frederick the Great (1712-1786) for a time, before he resigned.

GOOD TO KNOW

The Seven Years' War took place between 1756 and 1763 and was fought between France, Russia and Austria against Britain and Prussia. The clashes of this practically worldwide conflict took place on two theaters of operations:

- On the continent, Prussia successfully resisted the French, Russian and Austrian armies;
- In the American and Indian colonies, England defeated France.

The confrontation led to the Treaty of Paris, which marked the emergence of Prussia as the leading power and the decline of the French presence in North America and the East Indies.

Called back during the wars of the French Revolution, he retained the confidence of the Prussian King Frederick William II (1770-1840), despite his many defeats. A few years later, he emerged victorious from the War of the Sixth Coalition. As the commander of the Prussian troops in Belgium during the Hundred Days campaign, he was first defeated at Ligny, but managed to organize a disciplined retreat to Waterloo, where he participated in the defeat of Napoleon. Gebhard Leberecht Blücher died on 12 September 1819, in Krobielowice (Poland).

ANALYSIS OF THE BATTLE

PREPARATIONS

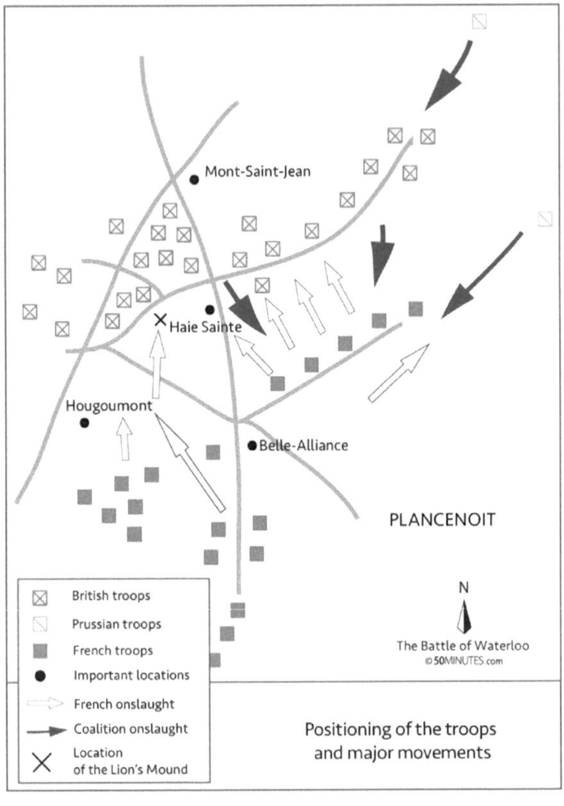

Positioning of the troops
and major movements

Coalition forces and Arthur Wellesley's plan

After the Prussian defeat at Ligny and the fighting between the British and the French at Quatre Bras, Arthur Wellesley decided to retreat to the plateau of Mont-Saint-Jean, south of Waterloo. There, he placed his troops in a strong defensive position on a broad front of 3 500 meters. He placed his men facing south across the Charleroi-Brussels road used by the French, forcing Napoleon I to fight at the place chosen by the commander of the allied troops.

Arthur Wellesley was at the head of an army of about 67 000 men (of whom 12 000 were horsemen) and possessed 159 pieces of artillery. The majority of the soldiers were British or Dutch, but there were also many German mercenaries. His battle plan was classic: he had a center and two wings and, from the front to the back, he kept an important reserve that could intervene if necessary. Moreover, the Prussian Marshal Gebhard Leberecht von Blücher, defeated at Ligny but who Napoleon did not pursue further, believing him to be definitively defeated, promised to join forces with Wellesley by strengthening the left side of the disposition. Relying on this help, the commander of the Allied forces placed his best troops on the right wing. He also took advantage of topography by placing his soldiers in a counter-slope to hide them from the eyes of the French and protect them from their artillery.

The French forces and Napoleon's plan

The French troops arrived on the battlefield in the evening of 17 June, but it was too late to commence the fight. Yet,

Napoleon I knew that he was running out of time, since he had to attack Arthur Wellesley's troops before they received reinforcements. He was confident, however, as he believed that the British were trying to gain time and that he would abort the fighting as soon as the French attacked.

The French emperor was at the head of 74 000 men (of whom 13 000 were horsemen) and held approximately 250 pieces of artillery. As was customary, Napoleon placed his troops in three levels, with the most advanced located to the right of the group – and thus facing Arthur Wellesley's left wing, which was the weakest. The numerical relationship between the two adversaries was roughly equal, but Napoleon nevertheless had more artillery.

Underestimating the determination of the allies, the Emperor planned a violent attack on the center and the left wing of his adversaries' disposition in order to achieve a quick victory. He appeared quite optimistic about the outcome of the battle. A few hours before the beginning of the hostilities, he told his officers: "We'll settle this matter by lunchtime; we shall sleep in Brussels tonight" (Bernard, 1973: p. 221).

THE FIRST ACT: THE FRENCH ATTACK

Unfortunately for Napoleon I, it rained on 18 June. It did not begin to clear until about 9am, but the Emperor decided to wait a little for the land to dry, which would facilitate his men's attack. He took advantage of this setback to review his troops and get them cheering.

Napoleon I on the battlefield.

In the opposing camp, Arthur Wellesley observed with his telescope and heard the cries of French soldiers cheering. But it took more to impress the British commander who calmly waited for the start of the attack, knowing that the more time passed, the closer the Prussians would be to the battlefield.

At 11:15am, Napoleon launched the attack. He ordered a diversionary attack on the right flank of the coalition (at the level of the castle-farm of Hougoumont) while he intended to have the bulk of his troops attack the other side. But his orders were misinterpreted, and what should have been a simple diversion became a vigorous assault. The situation was quickly deemed critical as Hougoumont was well defended, and the French were forced to send for reinforcements, which mobilized just under 10 000 men, who therefore did not participate in the actual attack.

Attack in Hougoumont.

The French artillery came in around noon and the bombing of the allied troops reached its peak between 1:30pm and 2pm, after which the bulk of Napoleon's troops rushed to attack the enemy positions. But while Arthur Wellesley's men had been relatively protected until then by their position, the advancing French were now severely affected by the British artillery, which included a new type of ammunition: the shrapnel (a shell that exploded before impact, simultaneously projecting many bullets). Arthur Wellesley decided to launch a part of his cavalry, which forced Napoleon's troops to retreat. In response, Napoleon gave the same orders: his cavalry almost destroyed that of his opponent. The cost of the first wave of attack was consequently costly on the side of the allies. However, Arthur Wellesley managed to withstand it.

At 3pm, Napoleon decided to conduct a general attack against the center of the British formation. The French artillery entered into action again, forcing Arthur Wellesley to pull back his troops. The French Marshal Michel Ney, believing the British were retreating, ordered the cavalry to charge. But, as in the first attack, the attackers were set back by the British artillery and then faced a powerful infantry. Napoleon was then forced to send reinforcements to help the French Marshal.

THE SECOND ACT: THE ARRIVAL OF THE PRUSSIANS

Warned of the arrival of Gebhard Leberecht Blücher's Prussian troops, the French emperor had taken care to send around ten thousand men to contain them at 1:30pm, hoping that this would leave him free to defeat Arthur Wellesley. But, the Prussians managed to outflank them and attacked the right wing of Napoleon's army at 4:30pm, so that he was obliged to send some of his reserve troops to curb the Prussian advance.

Putting his victory at stake, the French emperor ordered his men to capture the central position of Arthur Wellesley's army, located near the farm of La Haye Sainte, at all costs. Michel Ney led the attack and reached his objective at 6:30pm. Napoleon I seemed to be winning the battle, but the commander of the British troops resisted bravely: "My instructions? They could not be simpler: hold out until the very end" (Bernard, 1973: 232), he reportedly said, as he knew that time was in his favor and that, if his troops were still resisting even a little, the Prussians might bring him victory.

Charge of the French Cuirassiers at Waterloo, painting by Henry Félix Emmanuel Philippoteaux, 1874.

Taking advantage of his success, Marshal Michel Ney requested reinforcements from Napoleon I, who refused in order to preserve the remaining forces for the Prussian attack. Indeed, Gebhard Leberecht Blücher had just launched a series of onslaughts, threatening to pierce the right wing of the French. The Emperor, keeping only the Imperial Guard with him, directed his reserves towards the Prussians and, at around 7pm, the troops of Gebhard Leberecht Blücher were momentarily stopped and the French right flank stabilized.

THE THIRD ACT: THE ATTACK FROM THE COALITION

Believing the Prussians to be permanently immobilized and Arthur Wellesley's reserves exhausted, Napoleon launched his elite unit, the Imperial Guard, at 7:30pm. However, the situation of the coalition was not as dire as the Emperor had believed. The Prussian troops continued to join the battlefield and strengthened the left wing of the British commander, allowing Wellesley to bring some of his troops towards his center, which was considerably weakened.

Thanks to these reinforcements, the allied troops resisted the onslaught of the Imperial Guard and decided to counter-attack. The situation quickly became critical for the French: the front was weakened, some units retreated and defeat quickly turned into disaster. The soldiers fled in disarray, covered by the heroic resistance of some formations of the Guard, which stayed in a defensive square formation. According to legend, Jacques Pierre Étienne, Viscount of Cambronne (1770-1842), commander of the final square, responded to a British general who told him to surrender: "The Guard dies and does not surrender!"[1] (*Le mot de Cambronne*, [no date]). Although the British insisted his response became shorter and much less elegant: "Merde!" (*ibid*.). Shortly after, the fearless French soldier was captured.

At around 10 or 11pm that night, while Napoleon I fled the battlefield, Arthur Wellesley and Gebhard Leberecht Blücher met and celebrated their victory, while the newly arrived Prussians were in charge of pursuance.

THE BATTLE OF WATERLOO: OUTCOME AND CONTROVERSIES

From a human point of view, the Battle of Waterloo was extremely deadly, although it did not last more than a day. The British and Dutch losses amounted to around 17 000 dead and wounded and their Prussian allies lost around 7 000 men. The outcome was therefore costly and, even if he was victorious, Arthur Wellesley did not have the heart to celebrate: "With such losses, how can one expect me to feel the slightest joy in my victory?" (Bernard, 1973: 218).

Among the French, there were no less than 26 000 killed and wounded, along with a further 10 000 prisoners. Most of the healthy and sound French soldiers dispersed or deserted the conflict. Thus, of the 74 000 men that made up Napoleon I's army on the morning of 18 June, only 27 000 regrouped in Laon on 24 June. For the coalition, victory was

---

1. This quotation has been translated by 50Minutes.com.

therefore complete: Napoleon I could not continue to fight and was forced to abdicate a second time on 22 June 1815.

To explain the French defeat, several consequential errors can be highlighted:

- The transmission of orders was not always fast and accurate. This explains one reason why the intended diversion on Hougoumont turned into an aggressive attack. The same can be said for the attack from Michel Ney's cavalry, which took place at 3pm and was much too early according to Napoleon I. In both cases, the Emperor was forced to send reinforcements to support actions that he had not yet approved.
- Napoleon I also made an error when he chose to use his reserves to face the Prussian attack on the right flank, instead of providing support to Michel Ney who had just taken over the farm of La Haye Sainte and was asking for reinforcements to deal a fatal blow to the British. This allowed Arthur Wellesley to strengthen his center and thus to face the attack of the Imperial Guard.
- When the French captured artillery pieces from their opponents, they did not put them out of use. Therefore, each time the French retreated to prepare a new charge, Arthur Wellesley's troops were able to use them again.

However, the main mistake made by the French was failing to prevent the troops of Gebhard Leberecht Blücher from joining in Waterloo. In this regard, Napoleon I created a major controversy during his exile on the island of St. Helena by blaming Emmanuel, Marquis de Grouchy, who he sent on 17 June with 34 000 men in pursuit of the Prussians when they were beaten the day before at Ligny. Through this accusation, he was trying to hide that his victory on 16 June had perhaps made him a little too confident. Indeed, believing the Prussians were defeated and were fleeing to Namur, it was not until the following day at 1pm that he ordered Marquis de Grouchy to head towards Gembloux, then to Namur, with orders to monitor the retreat of Gebhard Leberecht Blücher or even, if necessary, to prevent him from joining the British. But the Emperor was mistaken: the Prussians, far from being dispirited by their defeat, managed to rally the British near Wavre on 17 June. As for Marquis de Grouchy, he reached Gembloux by the end of the day and, the following morning, he followed his orders to pursue the Prussians towards Wavre, which he would continue to do even when the first sounds of artillery action in Waterloo could be heard. But Gebhard Leberecht Blücher did not allow him to catch up with him and divided his troops in two: one group was sent to the aid of Arthur Wellesley, the other remained in Wavre to block the French Marshal and his 34 000 men, preventing them from joining the battlefield. When Marquis de Grouchy finally received the urgent order to go and assist the Emperor and strengthen his attack at around 5 or 7 o'clock that evening, he found himself trapped in Wavre in a standoff, without aim. Thus, although it is clear that Marquis de Grouchy did not possess the military genius of his leader, Napoleon also bears his share of the responsibility for the arrival of the Prussians at Waterloo and the absence of 34 000 of his men on the battlefield.

IMPACT OF THE BATTLE

The short and long-term repercussions of the Battle of Waterloo are numerous and extremely significant, since they constitute a real turning point in the history of Europe.

INTERNATIONAL CONSEQUENCES

In the short term, the defeat suffered by Napoleon I put a definitive end to his ambitions for domination of the European continent. As soon as he was defeated, he returned to Paris in the hope of rallying as many people as possible in order to continue the fight, but members of parliament forced him to abdicate again on 22 June 1815. Subsequently, after an unsuccessful attempt to leave for the United States, he surrendered to the British on 15 July. They exiled him as far as possible, on the island of St. Helena where he arrived in October 1815. He died there on 5 May 1821.

The victory of the coalition at Waterloo specifically marks the triumph of the principles of legitimacy and European balance. According to these two notions, the Four Great Powers (Great Britain, Russia, Austria and Prussia) reorganized Europe at the Congress of Vienna (September 1814-June 1815). Several decisions were made during this time:

- Firstly, the Powers denied the ideas of the Revolution. Monarchies were restored where the wars of the Revolution and of the Empire had abolished them. France therefore returned to a monarchy and Louis XVIII came to power.

- Then, on behalf of European balance, the map of Europe (and the rest of the world) was redrawn to establish a level of equality of forces between the major powers, in order to avoid new wars. Thus, Britain expanded into the Mediterranean basin and India; Russia obtained Finland and a part of Poland; Prussia also received a part of Poland and added Saxony and Rhineland to its possessions; Austria also took a part of Poland and annexed Tyrol and part of Northern Italy.
- Finally, believing that France was still a threat, the victors of the Battle of Waterloo created several buffer states around it to prevent France from invading its neighbors again. Among these were the United Kingdom of the Netherlands (consisting of what is known today as Belgium and the Netherlands) in the north and the Kingdom of Piedmont-Sardinia in the south-east.

By redrawing the map of Europe according to their wishes, the victors of Napoleon I did not take into account the desire for independence of some peoples (e.g. Poland). Putting aside the new ideas introduced by the Revolution (independence, freedom, equality, etc.), the selfishness of the Great Powers of Europe laid the foundations for the liberal revolutions that erupted in Europe in 1848 during the Spring of Nations.

CONSEQUENCES IN FRANCE

On 20 November 1815, following its defeat, France was forced to sign the Treaty of Paris, according to which the country:

- regained its borders from 1790 and therefore lost all the conquests acquired during the revolutionary and imperial periods;
- was forced to accept an army occupation on its soil for three years;
- had to pay large indemnities.

One should also consider the significant economic and demographic losses. Although Napoleon I conducted several economic reforms, in particular to allow France to improve its industrial potential, he departed from a ruined country in 1815. Due to the costs of the war, the large debt it generated and the indemnities it was forced to pay, France entered into a crisis that would take around 20 years to overcome. The country was also weakened demographically: it was estimated that approximately one million men died during the Napoleonic wars, creating a significant deficit, even though France remained the highest populated country in Europe.

THE DOMINATION OF GREAT BRITAIN

The victory of the coalition was primarily that of the British. Indeed, more than once, while the European continent was defeated by Napoleon I, Britain was the only one to resist, which may have been made easier due to its insular position. It was also due to British impulse that the seven successive coalitions were formed, as Britain did not hesitate to pay other states to enter the fight. Aware of the danger, Napoleon I very quickly tried to stop the British by ordering a continental blockade in 1806 to ruin them. But, thanks to their large fleet, the British took control of the seas, allowing them to bypass the blockade and continue trading with Russia, the Scandinavian countries and the United States.

The end of the Napoleonic period allowed Britain to assert itself as the leading world power, particularly in economic terms. Relying on a growing population and a vast colonial empire which supplied raw materials, Great Britain became the industrial, commercial and financial center of Europe, perhaps even of the world. To maintain that power, Britain developed a large fleet which was tasked with defending its empire and commerce around the world. Its influence also extended into the cultural field: the English language became international and the British way of life began to spread.

However, the 20th century brought an end to the golden age of the British: the First World War (1914-1918) from which Britain emerged victorious, but ruined, and the economic competition from the United States left Great Britain in the background.

MILITARY CONSEQUENCES

Arthur Wellesley's victory at Waterloo was primarily due to the superiority of his defensive organization in relation to the measures of attack implemented by Napoleon I. This battle marked a turning point in military history: gradually, the defense gained an advantage over the attack.

Indeed, Napoleon I specialized in large attacks that aimed to bring his armies to the right place at the right time in order to beat the enemy in close combat with quick, powerful strikes. However, in Waterloo, Arthur Wellesley cleverly arranged his troops in a strong defensive position that allowed him to resist all of the French assaults.

Following the battle, the defense became stronger than the attack, mainly due to technological progress (more powerful artillery, faster guns, etc.). This trend lasted more than 100 years and culminated in the First World War, during which hundreds of thousands of men rose to the assault of enemy trenches. It was not until World War II and the widespread use of armored vehicles that the trend reversed.

SUMMARY

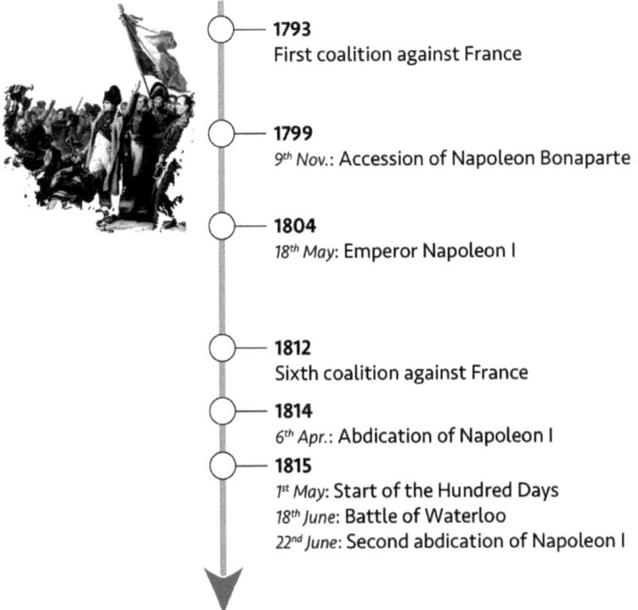

1793
First coalition against France

1799
9th Nov.: Accession of Napoleon Bonaparte

1804
18th May: Emperor Napoleon I

1812
Sixth coalition against France

1814
6th Apr.: Abdication of Napoleon I

1815
1st May: Start of the Hundred Days
18th June: Battle of Waterloo
22nd June: Second abdication of Napoleon I

- From 1793 to 1814, six successive coalitions of the great European powers fought Revolutionary and Napoleonic France.
- Defeated for the first time in 1814, Napoleon was forced into exile, but returned to France in March 1815, prompting the creation of a seventh coalition against him.
- On 15 June 1815, the Emperor entered Belgium with 125 000 men in order to separately defeat the Anglo-Dutch troops led by Arthur Wellesley (100 000 men) and

the Prussian troops led by Gebhard Leberecht Blücher (150 000 men).

- The following day, Napoleon I defeated the Prussians at Ligny and opened the road to Brussels in order to face the Anglo-Dutch at the Quatre Bras. Believing he had definitively beaten the troops of Gebhard Leberecht Blücher, Napoleon I pursued Arthur Wellesley, who had withdrawn his troops to a defensive position near Waterloo.

- On 18 June, in Mont-Saint-Jean, Arthur Wellesley had control of 67 000 men and 159 pieces of artillery entrenched in a strong defensive position. Napoleon launched into battle with 74 000 men and 250 pieces of artillery.

- The fight began at around 11am and the French attacks followed one after another to the point where, at around 7pm, the Anglo-Dutch troops were about to surrender. However, the Prussians, having escaped the troops later sent by the Emperor in pursuit, came out onto the battle-field and irremediably tipped the balance in favor of the coalition. At around 10pm or 11pm that night, the battle was over: Napoleon returned to France, defeated.

- Following this crushing defeat, the French emperor abdicated for a second time on 22 June 1815 and was permanently exiled to the island of St. Helena, where he died on 5 May 1821.

- Furthermore, Europe was reorganized according to the principles of legitimacy and European balance. Louis XVIII, a legitimate heir to the throne of France, was forced upon the French, while buffer states were created around France to maintain international stability. In addition to this, the victorious powers gave free reign to their ambitions and, in doing so, laid the foundations for the liberal revolutions of 1848.

- The battle also marked a significant decline of French power, exhausted by the Revolution and the Napoleonic period, and allowed Britain to assert itself as the leading world power.
- Finally, Waterloo was the beginning of a new chapter in military history, that of the defense's preeminence over the attackers, which was a trend that would later culminate in the First World War.

We want to hear from you!
Leave a comment on your online library
and share your favourite books on social media!

FIND OUT MORE

BIBLIOGRAPHY

- Barbero, A (2005) *Waterloo*. Paris: Flammarion.
- Bernard, H. (1973) *Le duc de Wellington et la Belgique*. Brussels: La Renaissance du Livre.
- Bruylants, A., De Callatay, P., Logie, J. and Pirenne, J.-H. (1990) *Waterloo 1815. L'Europe face à Napoléon*. Brussels: Crédit communal.
- Cyr, P. (2011) *Waterloo. Origines et enjeux*. Paris: L'Harmattan.
- Damamme, J.-C. (1999) *La bataille de Waterloo*. Paris: Perrin.
- D'Arjuzon, A. (1998) *Wellington*. Paris: Perrin.
- De Las Cases, E. (2008) *Mémorial de Sainte-Hélène*. Paris: Seuil.
- De Vos, L. (2002) *Four Days of Waterloo: 15th, 16th, 17th and 18th June 1815*. Louvain-la-Neuve: Versant Sud.
- De Waresquiel, E. (2008) *Cent Jours. La tentation de l'impossible. Mars-juillet 1815*. Paris: Fayard.
- Largeaud, J.-M. (2006) *Napoléon et Waterloo. La défaite glorieuse. De 1815 à nos jours*. Paris: La Boutique de l'Histoire.
- Logie, J. (1984) *Waterloo. L'évitable défaite*. Paris/Gembloux: Duculot.
- Logie, J. (2002) *Napoléon. La dernière bataille*. Brussels: Racine.
- Logie, J. (2005) *Waterloo: The Campaign of 1815*. Kent: Spellmount Ltd.
- Roberts, A. (2005) *Waterloo: Napoleon's Last Gamble*.

London: Harper Perennial.
- Tulard, J. (1985) *Napoleon: The Myth of the Saviour*. Trans. Waugh, T. London: Routledge.
- Tulard, J. (2012) *Napoléon, chef de guerre*. Paris: Tallandier.

ICONOGRAPHIC SOURCES

- Napoleon I on the battlefield. Royalty-free reproduction picture.
- Attack in front of Hougoumont. Royalty-free reproduction picture.
- Charge of the French Cuirassiers at Waterloo, painting by Henri Félix Emmanuel Philippoteaux, 1874. Royalty-free reproduction picture.

NOVELS

- Chateaubriand, F.-R. (2014) *Memoirs from Beyond the Tomb*. London: Penguin Classics.
- De Balzac, H. (2015) *The Country Doctor*. Trans. Marriage, E. CreateSpace Independent Publishing Platform.
- Doyle, A.C. (2016) *The Exploits of Brigadier Gerard*. CreateSpace Independent Publishing Platform.
- Hugo, V. (1982) *Les Misérables*. Trans. Denny, N. London: Penguin Classics.
- Southey, R. (2009) *The Poet's Pilgrimage to Waterloo*. BiblioLife Reproduction Series.

FILMS

- *Napoléon*. (1954) [Film]. Sacha Guitry. Dir. France/Italy: Les Films C.L.M., Film Sonor, Francinex, Rizzoli Film.
- *Waterloo*. (1970) [Film]. Sergueï Bondartchouk. Dir. Italy/Soviet Union: Mosfilm, Dino de Laurentiis, Cinematographica.
- *Napoléon*. (2002) [Television miniseries]. Yves Simoneau. Dir. France/Canada: A&E.

MUSEUMS AND COMMEMORATIVE BUILDINGS

- The Lion's Mound (*Butte du Lion*) in Waterloo (Belgium): This mound is 40 meters high and was erected on the battlefield, at the place where the Crown Prince of the United Kingdom of the Netherlands, William II, was wounded. A symbol of the victory of the coalition, the mound is topped with a statue of a lion (the emblem of the Netherlands) atop a stone pedestal, and is positioned facing towards France. At the top of the hill, a table of orientation provides some benchmark points about the battle.
- The Visitors Center and Panorama: Located next to the Lion's Mound, these two places are ideal starting points for a visit to the battle site. The Visitors Center shows two films that put the viewer at the heart of the events. The Panorama room contains a painting depicting the battle, objects from the period and sound effects that add to the atmosphere.
- The Wellington Museum: Located in the center of

Waterloo, the museum traces the story of the battle in detail and exhibits objects and weapons from the era.

- Napoleon's Last Headquarters: The museum is located on a farm where Napoleon spent the night of 16 to 17 June. It contains many souvenirs of the Emperor, as well as objects related to the Battle of Waterloo.
- The Wax Museum: Located near the Visitor's center, this museum showcases wax representations of key players in the battle.
- The Napoleonic Bivouacs: Every year in mid-June, a reconstruction of the army bivouacs takes place on the battlefield. This is an opportunity to discover the living conditions of the soldiers at the time, witness a reconstruction of the battles and see troop parades.
- The many memorials erected around the site of the battle.